THE POW

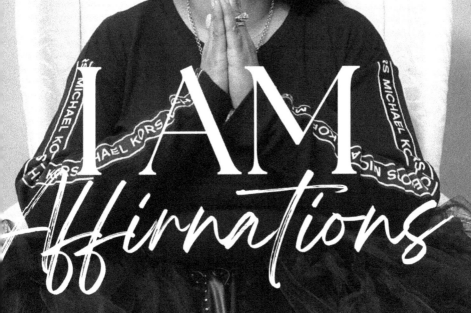

I AM
Affirmations

A DEVOTIONAL TO BUILDING YOUR INNER SELF VOLUME 1

DR. DIANE A. DUCKETT

The Power of I AM Affirmations:
A Devotional to Building Your Inner Self
Volume 1

Unless otherwise indicated, all Scripture quotations are taken from The Passion Translation® All Scripture quotations are from The Passion Translation®. Copyright © 2017, 2018, 2020 by Passion & Fire Ministries, Inc. Used by permission. All rights reserved. ThePassionTranslation.com. Scripture quotations marked NLT are from the Holy Bible, New Living Translation, copyright © 1996, used by permission of Tyndale House Publishers, Inc. Wheaton, Illinois 60189. Scripture quotations noted AMPLIFIED or AMP are taken from the Amplified® Bible, copyright © 1954, 1958, 1962, 1964, 1965, 1987 by The Lockman Foundation. Used by permission (www.Lockman.org). Scripture quotations marked ERV are taken from the Easy-to-Read Version (ERV), International Edition © 2013, 2016 by Bible League International and used by permission.

ISBN: 978-1-947741-83-6

Published by
Kingdom Publishing, LLC
1350 Blair Drive, Suite F, Odenton, MD 21113

Printed in the USA

Dedication

I dedicate this book to God, the Great I AM, who has given me the courage to write this devotional. To believe in myself that this book was in me and needed to come out of me. You allowed me to affirm within myself these I AM declaration of who I AM. Thank You God, the Great I AM for "Believing in Me!" I AM that I AM because of You, The Great I AM! I also, want to thank my Coach, Dr. Barbara A. Palmer who push me to complete this first volume of the I AM Affirmations Devotional.

Table of Contents

Foreword

It's important to the father that you speak words of affirmation over your life daily. His word teaches us that life and death are in the power of the tongue.

Dr. Diane Duckett's book of affirmations will strengthen your inner man and cause you to recognize who you are in Christ.

Why was it important for her to write this book of affirmations? Because she wanted you to discover, just as she did, the depths of the Father's love for you as you speak words of life over yourself.

Use this book of affirmations as a tool to smack the enemy in the face and remove negativity, doubt and fear!

-   Dr. Barbara A. Palmer, Pastor, Author, and Founder and CEO of Kingdom Kare, Inc., Odenton, MD

Preface

How to use this devotional. You will begin with the I AM statement. Each I AM statement has a scripture mediation. You will read the scripture mediation to help you connect to the I AM statement. Following the scripture mediation, there is a thought for today, which is actually the devotional. One you have read the thought for today you will pray the affirmation prayer. After praying the affirmation prayer, sit for a moment and think about the I AM statement. How did you connect with the I AM affirmation. Write down everything you are feeling about that affirmation.

Introduction

I'm so glad you've decided to grab this I AM affirmation devotional to building your inner self. I believe that speaking affirmations over your life is vital to your success. Did you know that speaking affirmations helps change the mindset of negative talk and negative thinking. The Bible tells us in Proverbs 23:7 (TPT) "For as he thinks within himself, so is he…" What you think about yourself will become your reality. This is why speaking positive affirmations to yourself daily is so vital, because it helps individuals to change the way they think about themselves. And what a powerful way to do so. Affirmation is the power of positive thinking that will help individuals change their thinking to live a better thoughtful life.

The Bible also tells us in Proverbs 10:11 (AMP) that "The mouth of the righteous is a fountain of life and his words of wisdom are a source of blessing…" Everyone wants a blessed life. But we must allow what we speak out of your mouth to become positive fruit in our lives. This is the fountain of life and your words will become a source of blessing when you speak positive affirmations over your life daily.

Did you know that our thoughts and words have formed our present and are currently forming our future? Every time we speak a word into the atmosphere, we bring life to that word. And if we are not careful, those words can affect us and others directly because of what was spoken. So be careful what you speak. For what you speak will manifest and become your reality.

Therefore, if we'd like to see real change in our life as well as success in our endeavors, we must change our mindset, re-program our thoughts and keep them positive – especially the thoughts about ourselves!" It is important to use these "I AM" affirmations to affirm the true essence of who you are. These I AM affirmations will give you a lift in spirit and a declaration to finally know your "I AM."

"I AM" is one of the most powerful statements we can make. Because when we use the words "I AM," we are saying, I AM what I think I AM. Thus, whatever follows "I AM" starts the creation of whatever you're claiming you are. The I AM is a pure statement of creation. God used I AM statements to declare who He is and who He is to us.

God states, His I AM declarations. He declares I AM the Alpha and Omega, I AM the Beginning and the End, I AM the Great I AM, I AM the Bread of Life, I AM the Lilly of the Valley, I AM the Bright and Morning Star, I AM All Powerful, I AM All Knowing, I AM who I say that I AM, I AM El-Shaddai – God Almighty, I AM the God of your father Abraham, I AM with you and will bless you, I AM Yahweh – the Lord, I AM the Lord who heals, I AM merciful, I AM slow to anger, I AM the Lord your God, I AM God, I AM the one who comforts, I AM a God who is near, I AM the Messiah, I AM the Light of the World, I AM the good shepherd, I AM the way, the Truth and the Life, I AM the Resurrection and the Life, I AM the One who Is and was and is coming, I AM coming soon, I AM. How powerful is that? God, knows who He is! I feel the power of I AM just by speaking God's I AM's out loud. That's the power of I AM statements. You will feel more empowered, more inspired when you used I AM affirmations and declare them over your life. Begin speaking these affirmations over your life:

I AM Redeemed

I AM Forgiven

I AM Loved

I AM Healthy

I AM Wealthy

I AM the Head and not the Tail

I AM Above and not Beneath

I AM A Child of God

I AM Royal Priest, a Holy Nation

I AM A Kings Kid

I AM Valuable

I AM Strong

I AM Significant

I AM Chosen by God!

I AM COMPLEX and BREATHTAKING

Scripture Meditation

"You formed my innermost being, shaping my delicate inside and my intricate outside, and wove them all together in my mother's womb. I thank you, God, for making me so mysteriously complex! Everything you do is marvelously breathtaking. It simply amazes me to think about it!"
Psalms 139:13-14 (TPT)

Thought For Today

I AM mysteriously complex! I AM marvelously breathtaking!

I love this Psalm, because David recognizes his I AM. I AM mysteriously complex! I AM marvelously breathtaking! David here is depicting in this Psalm how God truly knows about us. Many times, we question our makeup. We question all the things we don't like about ourselves or about what others think of us. So sometimes we question if we are wonderfully made, because we base it off our flawed selves. Yet, by nature we are flawed vessels, but when God created us, there was no flaw in His work of creating us. And I believe that's why the Psalmist penned this Psalm, so we could understand that although we may think we are flawed and others may think we are flawed, God doesn't think so. We are mysteriously complex and marvelously breathtaking and God knows all about you and I.

How does He know about you? God sees and knows everything that occurs in the conception and development of human life as it is carefully and skillfully embroidered in the darkness of the womb. When you were in your mother's womb, He cared so much about you that He began to delicately shape you inside the darkness of your mother's womb, woven you together, forming your eyes, ears, nose, lips, face, legs, feet, hands, smile, sex and even down to the color of your skin, so that you could be breathtaking when you arrived. Isn't that how it is when a mother carries a child for nine months and when the day arrives and the baby is born, the baby is breathtaking. So breathtaking that everyone can't wait to see it. Oh, the joy of being mysteriously complex and marvelously breathtaking by God.

I can imagine that God intentionally created nine months of pregnancy for that very reason. To show us that life just does not happen, but life takes time. Because there has to be a forming and a shaping. And if you are wondering if you are mysteriously complex and marvelously breathtaking – know that you are. Never allow anyone to tell you otherwise. You are mysteriously complex! You are marvelously breathtaking. You are the greatest miracle God created and that's worth getting excited about. It simply amazes me to think about it. And because of the work His done on you through the forming and the shaping, He knows you, because He created you to be the person you are today.

So go ahead and own your I AM! Because your I AM has given you the gift of being mysteriously complex and marvelously breathtaking by God who truly knows all about you.

Affirmation Prayer

Lord, today I affirm that you know all about me. Lord, you know everything there is to know about me. You perceive every movement of my heart and soul, and you understand my every thought before it even enters my mind. You are so intimately aware of me, Lord. You read my heart like an open book and you know all the words I'm about to speak before I even start a sentence! You know every step I will take before my journey even begins. You've gone into my future to prepare the way, and in kindness you follow behind me to spare me from the harm of my past. With your hand of love upon my life, you impart a blessing to me. This is just too wonderful, deep, and incomprehensible! Your understanding of me brings me wonder and strength.

Thank you, Lord for empowering me, by forming my innermost being, and shaping my delicate inside and my intricate outside, and knitting them together in my mother's womb.

Thank you, Lord, for making me mysteriously complex!

Thank you, Lord that everything you do is marvelously breathtaking.

Lord, I affirm that I AM Fearfully and Wonderfully Made! I AM Complex and I AM Breathtaking! I declare and decree this over my life today! In Jesus Name. Amen!

Connect with your I AM

Are you a complex person? If yes, explain.

_____

_____

_____

_____

_____

How does God know about you?

_____

_____

_____

_____

_____

What does God think about you?

_____

_____

_____

_____

_____

Do you see what God sees about you? If so, explain.

_____

_____

_____

_____

_____

What is one thing you will embrace about this I AM affirmation?

_____

_____

_____

_____

How will you embrace it?

_____

_____

_____

_____

How have you connected with this I AM?

_____

_____

_____

_____

_____

_____

_____

_____

I AM DESTINY

Scripture Meditation

"We have become his poetry, a recreated people that will fulfill the destiny he has given each of us, for we are joined to Jesus, the Anointed One. Even before we were born, God planned in advance our destiny and the good works we would do to fulfill it!"
Ephesians 2:10 (TPT)

Thought For Today

Ephesians 2:10 paints a beautiful picture of God's creation for each of us. Here in vs.10 The Passion Translations tells us that we have become his poetry. In the Greek word poetry used here is translated "poem" or "poetry." What is a poem? It is *"a piece of writing that partakes of the nature of both speech and song that is nearly always rhythmical, usually metaphorical, and often exhibits such formal elements as meter, rhyme, and stanzaic structure."* This means that God as the artist seeks to express Himself in his work that is rhythmical. There is a rhythm to what God wants to express in us and through us concerning our destiny. We are not just a recreated people, but also a recreated people with a purpose, where God is expressing Himself in you. You are His workmanship, you are His poem. This means that our lives are the beautiful poetry written by God that will speak forth all that he desires for us in life.

God has a special plan for your life. He created you with a specific purpose in mind to fulfill the destiny He has for you. Ephesians 2:10 is an astonishing passage that not only reveals the special care God took to make our lives beautiful, but also to design the very good works that we are supposed to do. If you are feeling bad about your life and believe destiny

13

is not in you, think again, because Ephesians 2:10 describes God's purpose for our lives. He has designed it to make you purposeful.

Your purpose is filled with a destiny that was created an advance by God for me to do. Sometimes the enemy will make you believe that you have no purpose and there's no destiny for your life. What the enemy will have you believe is not what God thinks or says about you. You must believe that God's hand is on your life. Know that God wants to display in you and through you His good works, His purpose and His destiny that He planned an advance for you to do and accomplish. You have purpose and you have destiny. You have become His poetry, recreated to fulfill destiny, because you are joined with the Anointed One Jesus, who was also created with a purpose and a destiny to do good works.

So don't allow anyone to tell you that there's no destiny or purpose in you. YES! THERE IS A PURPOSE AND A DESTINY WAITING FOR YOU TO REALIZE YOU HAVE IT WITHIN YOU! The very plan that God created you to do, was a plan to give you purpose, destiny, and success. And that success is your purpose colliding with your destiny surrounded by the good works He planned an advance for you to do. Therefore, success is within you with a purpose, colliding with your destiny. And so today, you must declare "I AM Destiny!" Because God created you to fulfill a destiny, which He prepared an advance for you to do.

Affirmation Prayer

God, today I affirm that I AM Destiny. God, thank you for allowing me to become your poetry, a recreated people that will fulfill the destiny you have given me, for I am joined to Your Son Jesus, the Anointed One. Even before I was born, God, you planned an advance my destiny, and the good works I would do to fulfill it. My destiny is to be successful in that which you purpose me for. No matter what the enemy says, I believe your word and the promises of your word. I affirm that I AM Destiny, a poetry, recreated to fulfill the destiny you have given me. Thank you, God for purpose and destiny.

Today, I affirm I AM DESTINY! I AM DESTINY! I AM DESTINY! I declare and decree this affirmation over my life today! In Jesus Name. Amen!

Connect with your I AM

What do you already know about what you were made to do?

_____

_____

_____

_____

_____

What has your life experience told you about your destiny?

_____

_____

_____

_____

_____

What relationships or people have influenced your sense of destiny?

_____

_____

_____

_____

_____

What does God say about your destiny?

_____

_____

_____

_____

_____

_____

How will you embrace your destiny?

_____

_____

_____

_____

_____

_____

_____

How have you connected with this I AM?

_____

_____

_____

_____

_____

_____

_____

_____

_____

_____

_____

I AM READY FOR WHAT IS COMING!

Scripture Meditation

"For I am about to do something new. See, I have already begun! Do you not see it? I will make a pathway through the wilderness. I will create rivers in the dry wasteland."
Isaiah 43:19 (NLT)

Thought For Today

Have you ever been ready for something? I mean, really, really ready? You've been patiently waiting on the sideline for your name to be called. To say, you're up next. I know waiting can be nerve recking. It can be frustrating. It can mess with your emotions. And I get that. But did you know that waiting is good thing. Because in the waiting, you are being prepared for your readiness. You are being equipped for your readiness. You are being shaped and molded for your readiness.

The moment you know you are ready for something new it will be a pivotal moment in your life. When you are ready for something new, something different, you will begin to since and feel your readiness, because it will be loud and undeniable. The scripture tells us, "For I am about to do something new. See, I have already begun! Are you ready for something new?

Ready! Ready! I Am Ready for what is coming. Do you see it! Do you not perceive it! It's on its way to you. So, believe it. You've been asking and waiting. Asking and waiting. So here it comes ready to meet you. Are you ready for the outpouring! Are you ready for the blessing! Are you ready to shine bright, light a diamond! Ready! Ready! I AM ready for what is coming! Lift up your hands and receive the ready blessings coming your way. Because it's on its way to meet you. It's not far. It's just around the corner. Are you ready! Affirm to yourself today, I AM Ready to take charge of my life! I AM Ready to tear down barriers that hold me back! I AM Ready to embrace and own my success! I AM Ready to show up for me! I AM Ready to become, embrace and thrive! I AM Ready! Ready! Ready! I AM ready for what is coming!

Affirmation Prayer

God, today I affirm that I AM Ready for what is coming! I AM Ready for whatever you have in store for me. God, I believe you are about to do something new in my life. You, God, are making a pathway through the wilderness. You, God, are creating rivers in dry places. You, God, are doing something that I AM Ready and prepared for. God, I AM Ready for what is coming. Thank you in advance for something new. In Jesus Name! Amen.

Connect with your I AM

What is the something new you ready for?

_____

_____

_____

_____

_____

How do you know you are ready for something new?

_____

_____

_____

_____

_____

What has been revealed to you about your readiness?

_____

_____

_____

_____

Is there anything holding you back from moving towards your readiness?

_____

_____

_____

_____

_____

What can you do to change this?

_____

_____

_____

_____

How are you becoming ready? What steps have/are you taking to become ready?

_____

_____

_____

_____

_____

How have you connected with this I AM?

_____

_____

_____

I AM MY WORDS

Scripture Meditation

"Your words have the power to bring great blessing: 'The mouth of the good person is a deep, life giving well'"
Proverbs 10:11-12 (TPT)

Thought For Today

I AM My Words is an affirmation that we don't recognize much when words are spoken out of our mouth. You see, words are powerful and effective. Whatever you speak out of your mouth will ultimately become your reality. As the scripture states, "Your words have the power to bring great blessing..." Do you want to see great blessings pour into your life because of how you've changed the words that are coming out of your mouth?

Never speak words that you do not want to become a seed in your life. Because every word that is spoken, rather negative or positive becomes a seed, and once it becomes a seed, it begins to grow as you continue to water it. Every time you open your mouth and speak a word, those words become a life giving well, springing forth the words that you spoke. This is why whenever you speak a word, it should be life-giving, refreshing, encouraging, empowering, and inspiring. Your words should edify, uplift, and empower you.

The words you say to yourself, and the words you put into the atmosphere, should be in alignment and harmony to what you want your life to look like. When you know the power of your words, your words will bring great blessings. Speak only that which you want to show up in your life. Because "The mouth of the good person is a deep, life giving well." Always speak life into your life! Period

Declare to yourself today, I AM My Words! My words have the power to bring me great blessings. Today, I speak only positive words that will empower my life. Today, I speak only words that I want to see manifest in my life. Today, I choose words that will only empower, inspire, edify, and encourage. Because I now know that what I speak will become my reality. I AM My Words.

SAY THIS WITH ME...

I AM MY WORDS!
I AM POWERFUL!
I AM FRUITFUL!
I AM BLESSED!
I AM HIGHLY FAVORED!
I AM A CHAMPION!
I AM A WINNER!
I AM SET APART!

I create whatever I speak, and whatever I speak, I will have.
Whatever I decide to be, I will be.
The evidence is all around me.
The power of my words has brought me precisely to where I am right now.

I have made the choices. I have held the thoughts.
I have taken the actions to create my current reality by using the words I speak. And I have the power to change it into whatever I want it to be.
I speak life, over every area of my life. My family, My finances, My career, My health, My friendships, My business, and even my attitude.

I speak God's promises always in my life, because I AM MY WORDS!

Affirmation Prayer

God, today I affirm that I AM MY WORDS. The words that I speak out of my mouth are life given, powerful, and will become a great blessing.

From this day forward, I will only speak words that are encouraging, inspiring, and positive into my atmosphere. My words will now become in alignment with what I want my reality to be. Because I AM my words and my words are who I am today. I declare and decree this affirmation over my life today! In Jesus Name. Amen!

Connect with your I AM

Are you a product of your words? If so, how?

_____

_____

_____

_____

What words have you spoken into the atmosphere that has shaped part or all of your reality?

_____

_____

_____

_____

Does these words empower and edify you?

_____

_____

_____

_____

What does God say about how you think and speak?

_____

_____

_____

_____

_____

How can you change the way you think and speak?

_____

_____

_____

_____

List some steps you will take to change how you think and speak.

_____

_____

_____

_____

How have you connect with this I AM?

_____

_____

_____

_____

_____

_____

_____

_____

_____

I AM LIGHT

"Your lives light up the world. Let others see your light from a distance, for how can you hide a city that stands on a hilltop? And who would light a lamp and then hide it in an obscure place? Instead, it's placed where everyone in the house can benefit from its light. So don't hide your light! Let it shine brightly before others, so that the commendable things you do will shine as light upon them, and then they will give their praise to your Father in heaven."
Matthew 5:14-16 (TPT)

Thought For Today

I AM Light! When I think about light. I think about light as life giving. Because light exposes. Light illuminates. Light makes things visible. For example, the sun brings light to the world. The switch that you flip to turn on the light helps you to see better, or clearly. Light is such a powerful source that we often take for granted. Not only the actual physical light, but the light within you. You see, if you really understood the light within you, you would not have to hide it. How many times have you hidden the light within you, because you truly did not want to stand out in the crowd or from a distance?

Can I tell you God wants you to shine brightly and declare the light that is within you. Because the light that is within you is so powerful, it can change your atmosphere and people who enter your space. I remember, when I was working for the government, every time I went into the office it was always dark. My coworker for some reason liked working in the dark. And for me, I could not work in the dark. Why, because working in the dark was a sign of depression and sadness. And I surely did not want to feel depression, nor sadness. So, I would come in to work and turn all the lights on. My co-workers would tell me it is so bright in here, can we turn the lights down. My response was absolutely not. It's too dark in here, and I need to see what I am doing while working. So, one day, my boss comes out of her office and shares with me. "You know, since you've been here, the office has been different. There is more laughter. People are coming in happy. They are even talking to one other, which never happened. You brought light into this office that we've never had before." Just by turning on the light made a big difference in the atmosphere and in the people. Never dim your light for anyone, because you are light that can brighten dark places.

When we shine our light, we shine Jesus who is the light of the world. When He is in us, His light shines through us beaming that light out to the world. Today, declare, I AM Light! because you are light to atmospheres and to people.

Affirmation Prayer

God, today I affirm that I AM Light. My life lights up the world. And others see my light from a distance, for how can I hide a city that stands on a hilltop? And who would light a lamp and then hide it in an obscure place? Instead, it's placed where everyone in the house can benefit from its light. So don't hide your light! Let it shine brightly before others, so that the commendable things you do will shine as light upon them, and then they will give their praise to your Father in heaven. I declare and decree this affirmation over my life today! In Jesus Name. Amen!

Connect with your I AM

How are you becoming the light in your environment?

_____

_____

_____

Does others recognize the light you bring to their environment? How so?

_____

_____

_____

_____

_____

Write about a time someone shared with you that light you bring when you are around.

_____

_____

_____

_____

_____

_____

_____

_____

_____

_____

_____

_____

_____

_____

How have you connected with this I AM?

_____
_____
_____
_____
_____
_____
_____
_____
_____
_____
_____
_____
_____
_____
_____
_____
_____
_____
_____
_____
_____
_____
_____
_____
_____
_____
_____

I AM One with God

*I pray for them all to be joined together as one even as you and I,
Father, are joined together as one. I pray for them to become one with us
so that the world will recognize that you sent me.*
John 17:21 (TPT)

Thought For Today

Jesus expresses here in John 17 a prayer of oneness. What is oneness? According to the *Oxford Language Dictionary, "Oneness is the fact or state of being unified or whole, though comprised of two or more parts."* In this prayer, Jesus wanted all people to have a mutual indwelling of God. To have our state of being become unified, whole, one with God. I am in God, God is in you, you are in God, we are in each other. We are one with God, and God is in you. You see, you have to know that you are one with God. Being one with God should be the highlight of your life. And you must declare that over your life daily, until you are able to confidently say, I AM One with God, and God is with me. I AM that I AM, and I AM lives within me.

Today, declare: I AM one with God and God is with me. I AM aware of my oneness with Him. Know matter where I AM, God is near. I AM Present with Him. I AM Aligned with Him. I AM in Harmony with Him. I AM One with God, and God is with me. No matter what I AM up against, I feel His presence all around me. Nothing can shake me. Nothing can take me, because I AM One with God, and God is with me.

Affirmation Prayer

God, today I affirm that I AM One with God, and God is with me. Thank you for the reminder of scripture, I pray for them all to be joined together as one even as you and I, Father, are joined together as one. I pray for them to become one with us so that the world will recognize that you sent me. Thank you, God for allowing me to experience oneness with You. I declare and decree this affirmation over my life today! In Jesus Name.

Connect with your I AM

What is oneness?

_____

_____

_____

_____

_____

What does it mean to you to be one with God?

_____

_____

_____

_____

_____

How have you become one with God?

_____

_____

_____

_____

If you are not one with God, what steps can you take to become one with God?

_____

_____

_____

_____

How can you help others to become one with God?

_____

_____

_____

_____

How have you connected with this I AM?

_____

_____

_____

_____

_____

_____

_____

_____

_____

_____

_____

_____

_____

_____

I AM A FRIEND OF GOD

Scripture Meditation

"And the Scripture was fulfilled which says, "Abraham believed God, and this [faith] was credited to him [by God] as righteousness and as conformity to His will," and he was called the friend of God."
James 2:23 AMP

Thought For Today

I am reminded of the song, "I AM A Friend of God." As this song rings in my spirit, I believe God is reminding me that I AM a friend of God, He calls me friend. Not an associate, not a partner, but a friend. A friend who sticks closer than a brother, father, sister, mother, spouse. You see, Abraham believed God and because He believed God, He was called a friend of God. To be a friend of God, you must believe God in every area of your life to be called a friend of God. Because by faith, Abraham believed God even when he did not know what the outcome would be. Do you believe that you are a friend of God?

Jesus reminds his disciples, "You are my friends if you do what I command you" (John 15:14). Being a friend of God means your loyalty is to God. You walk in obedience to God. You trust God. If you are doing all of this, doing what He commands, you too can declare, I AM A Friend of God.

Affirmation Prayer

God, today I affirm that I AM A Friend of God, because I trust you. I obey you. I follow you. Thank you for being a friend and calling me friend. I AM A Friend of God. I declare and decree this affirmation over my life today! In Jesus Name. Amen!

Connect with your I AM

What kind of friend is God to you?

_____

_____

_____

_____

_____

Explain what a friend is?

_____

_____

_____

_____

_____

What does Jesus say about being a friend?

_____

_____

_____

_____

Are you that kind of friend? If so, how?

_____

_____

_____

_____

_____

_____

How can you become a better friend?

_____

_____

_____

_____

_____

How have you connected with this I AM

_____

_____

_____

_____

_____

_____

_____

_____

_____

_____

_____

_____

_____

_____

_____

_____

_____

_____

I AM FRUITFUL

Scripture Meditation

"Stay joined to me and I will stay joined to you. No branch can produce fruit alone. It must stay connected to the vine. It is the same with you. You cannot produce fruit alone. You must stay joined to me."
John 15:4 (TPT)

Thought For Today

Everyone loves success, abundance and prosperity. We all love to be fruitful and although we all want fruitfulness, very few understand the secret or the sequence to enjoy such a life. Jesus gives us the key to being fruitful. He states here in John 15:4, "stay joined to me and I will stay joined to you." It's just that simple, to becoming fruitful. If you want to be fruitful, you must stay joined to Him.

Sometimes being fruitful is a hard thing to do for many, simply because we focus on what others think of us verse what we think of ourselves. We want to be joined to what others think and are doing, verses staying joined to Jesus. Jesus says, if you stay joined to me, I will stay joined to you. When you stay joined to me, I will make you fruitful.

Don't you know, no branch, no person can produce fruit alone. Just like a grapevine. A grapevine cannot produce grapes if it's not connected to its source. Its source is being planted in the right kind of soil. If it is not planted in the right kind of soil, it can take years for it to produce grapes. That's why it needs to be connected to the right source for it to produce fruit. It's just like you and I, we cannot call ourselves fruitful if we don't stay connected and joined to the source who makes us fruitful.

Jesus wants you to say, "I AM Fruitful!" You should be able to say, "I AM Fruitful, because you are joined to Him and He is joined to you. You're not the branch that does not produce fruit, but you are the branch that is fruitful, since you are joined to something greater than yourself, who is Jesus. That's something to shout about! You are Fruitful, because you are joined to something greater than yourself and that greater is joined to you. That's why you are fruitful.

Affirmation Prayer

Father, today I affirm that I AM Fruitful. Your word tells us to stay joined to Your Son Jesus and He will stay joined to us. Father, we know that we cannot produce fruit alone, but we must stay connected to the vine, which is Your Son Jesus. So, Father, thank you for allowing us to be joined to Jesus and Him to us. Help us to affirm daily that we are fruitful because of it. I AM Fruitful! I declare and decree this affirmation over my life today! In Jesus Name. Amen!

Connect with your I AM

What does Jesus say about being fruitful?

_____

_____

_____

_____

_____

How does one become fruitful?

_____

_____

_____

_____

_____

_____

_____

How does one stay fruitful?

_____

_____

_____

_____

What are the qualities of being fruitful?

_____

_____

_____

_____

Are you in the fruitful category? If so, explain your answer.

_____

_____

_____

_____

How have you produced fruit that will last?

_____

_____

_____

_____

_____

_____

_____

How have you connected with this I AM?

_____

_____

_____

_____

_____

_____

_____

_____

_____

_____

_____

_____

_____

_____

_____

_____

_____

_____

_____

_____

_____

_____

_____

_____

I AM CONFIDENT

Scripture Meditation

I can do all things [which He has called me to do] through Him who strengthens and empowers me [to fulfill His purpose—I am self-sufficient in Christ's sufficiency; I am ready for anything and equal to anything through Him who infuses me with inner strength and confident peace.]
Philippians 4:13 (AMP)

Thought For Today

What do you rely on to give you confidence? Is it your will, or desire? Is it your talents and abilities? Is it your degrees and your accomplishments? Whatever the case maybe, we all gain confidence from someone or something. When we look at the word confidence, confidence can be defined as the feeling or belief that one can rely on someone or something. I remember when I was looking to buy a car. I really needed a new car, because my car at the current time was not fix. That car gave me so many problems. Every time I turned around something needed to be fixed and was causing me to pay more money to fix problems that would continue to become a problem.

So, one day, I told myself, "I'm getting a new car." I did not know how I was going to get a new car, but I just knew a new car was in my future. I began to visualize myself driving the new car and was very excited about it. One day I decided to go check my credit score. As I was checking my credit score, I saw a button that say click here to see if you qualify for a new car. I clicked the button, began putting in all of my information and the next thing I know, I was approved to purchase a new car. The app then proceeded to give me a recommendation on where I could purchase a new car. I click on the button and it allowed me to choose what I wanted to pay each month. I then proceed to look for the car of my choice in my price range. I was so nervous, because I really did not know if this was going to work out for me. I saw the car, and clicked to purchase. It notified me that I would receive confirmation of approved in about 3 business days. When I left the app, I started to claim my new car. I started to believe that the car was mines. About a half hour later, I was sent an email stating I was approved, when would you like to pick up your car. Do you know, I started screaming, shouting, and praising God! I litterly manifested a car within an hour. Glory hallelujah!

I was able to manifest the car, because God empowered me and fulfilled a purpose of something that I needed, not wanted, but needed. When we have confidence, we can see God in everything. God knows what we need, when we need it. If it's a new job you are looking for, be confidence. If it's a new car you are needing, be confidence. If it's to establish healthy relationships, be confident. If it's starting that new business, be confident. Declare to yourself today, *"I can do all things [which He has called me to do] through Him who strengthens and empowers me [to fulfill His purpose—I am self-sufficient in Christ's sufficiency; I am ready for anything and equal to anything through Him who infuses me with inner strength and confident peace."* Know that God has confidence, so much confidence in you.

Declare today, I AM Confident that I will succeed. I AM Confident that my conditions will improve. I AM Confident that I will get the job. I AM Confident that I will succeed in something.

Affirmation Prayer

God, today I affirm that I AM Confident. For your word states, *"I can do all things [which He has called me to do] through Him who strengthens and empowers me [to fulfill His purpose—I am self-sufficient in Christ's sufficiency; I am ready for anything and equal to anything through Him who infuses me with inner strength and confident peace."* God thank you for strengthening and empowering me to fulfill Your purpose You have for my life. Allow me to always be confident, knowing that you are working it out on my behalf. Thank God, inner strength and confident peace. I AM Confident!

I declare and decree this affirmation over my life today! In Jesus Name. Amen!

Connect with your I AM

What does confidence look like to you?

_____

_____

_____

_____

_____

What do you need confidence in to accomplish?

_____

_____

_____

_____

What steps will you take to gain the confidence you need today?

_____

_____

_____

_____

_____

_____

_____

_____

Are there any obstacles that keep you from being confident? If so, what are they?

_____

_____

_____

_____

_____

How can you show up with confidence today?

_____

_____

_____

_____

_____

_____

_____

_____

_____

_____

_____

_____

_____

_____

_____

_____

_____

_____

I AM INFLUENTIAL

Scripture Meditation

"Daniel soon proved himself more capable than all the other administrators and princes. Because of his great ability, the king made plans to place him over the entire empire. Then the other administrators and princes began searching for some fault in the way Daniel was handling his affairs, but they couldn't find anything to criticize. He was faithful and honest and always responsible."
Daniel 6:3-4 NLT

Thought For Today

A lot of people want influence, yet few people have influence. The different in people wanting and people having influence is simply a commitment. A commitment to stay the course even if it's not popular. A commitment to not waver, even when others will. A commitment to stand true to one's values and belief, even when others will bend. Influence comes by way of commitment.

The online dictionary states the mean of commitment. *"Commitment is the state or quality of being dedicated to a cause, or activity."* Synonyms for commitment are *dedication, devotion, loyalty, faithfulness, responsibility, obligation, duty, etc.* In biblical terms, according to Open the Bible, *"Commitment means that certain decisions are made in advance. Irrespective of the circumstances: "I will honor Christ. Whatever the pain and whatever the cost. I will obey God's word, even when that is the hardest thing to do."* This was Daniel's commitment to obey whatever the cost.

I love Daniel's story. Daniel is a special person who was truly able to understand his commitment to God. You see, Daniel's commitment was living a life pleasing to God. Obeying God's every command. This life

42

gave him influence amongst kings, nations and people. His influence was impactful due to his commitment of living a life pleasing to God. Daniel was a man who spent quality time with God. His outward life was a direct reflection of the time he diligently spent in the presence of God. And his relationship with God would cause the king to think and do something different, especially after witnessing Daniel come out of the lion's den untouched. Daniel had to face the lion den simply because he would not obey the command giving by the king to not prayer to any gods for 30 days. Daniel knew where his influence came from and it was not from the other gods that others prayed to. No Daniel prayed to His God, the All Knowing and Powerful God. He knew what his relationship was to God. For this, God gave him influence amongst men.

How is your relationship with God? When we reflect on our relationship with God, does it show a commitment to living a life pleasing to God? Your commitment to living a life pleasing to God will be use to give you influence in your life. And God's influence in your life will show as you spend time in God's presence and in His Word.

Affirmation Prayer

God, today I affirm that I AM Influential! I want to make a commitment to you to always live to please you and all that I do. God, help to always remind committed to You by being faithful and honest and always responsible. And as I stay committed to you, help me to clearly see the places where I can have the greatest influence. Give me the courage, grace, and wisdom to speak into other's lives and reflect Your love that I might make an impact in the lives you bring me to, because I AM Influential and will make an impact wherever I go because my relationship with You.

I declare and decree this affirmation over my life today! In Jesus Name. Amen!

Connect with your I AM

How was Daniel influential?

_____

_____

_____

_____

_____

What did Daniel do to become influential?

_____

_____

_____

_____

What are some character traits Daniel had in becoming influential?

_____

_____

_____

_____

Like Daniel, what does God's influence in your life show?

_____

_____

_____

_____

How have you become influential?

_____

_____

_____

_____

_____

_____

How have you connected with this I AM?

_____

_____

_____

_____

_____

_____

_____

_____

_____

_____

_____

_____

_____

_____

_____

_____

_____

_____

_____

_____

_____

Powerful Scriptures to Start Your Day

Philippians 4:13 (AMP)
I can do all things [which He has called me to do] through Him who strengthens and empowers me [to fulfill His purpose—I am self-sufficient in Christ's sufficiency; I am ready for anything and equal to anything through Him who infuses me with inner strength and confident peace.]

Isaiah 54:17 (AMP)
No weapon that is formed against you will succeed; And every tongue that rises against you in judgment you will condemn. This [peace, righteousness, security and triumph over opposition] is the heritage of the servants of the Lord, and this is their vindication from Me," says the Lord.

Deuteronomy 28:13 (AMP)
The LORD will make you the head (leader) and not the tail (follower); and you will not be beneath, if you listen and pay attention to the commandments of the LORD your God, which I am commanding you today, to observe them carefully.

Philippians 4:19 (AMP)
And my God will liberally supply (fill until full) your every need according to His riches in glory in Christ Jesus.

Ephesians 3:30 (TPT)
Never doubt God's mighty power to work in you and accomplish all this. He will achieve infinitely more than your greatest request, your most unbelievable dream, and exceed your wildest imagination! He will outdo them all, for his miraculous power constantly energizes you.

Powerful Scriptures for Success in Life

Jeremiah 29:11 NIV
For I know the plans I have for you," declares the LORD," plans to prosper you and not to harm you, plans to give you hope and a future.

Psalm 5:3 ERV
Every morning, LORD, I lay my gifts before you and look to you for help. And every morning you hear my prayers.

Psalm 37:23-24 TPT
When Yahweh delights in how you live your life, he establishes your every step. If they stumble badly they will survive, for the Lord lifts them up with his hands.

Psalm 23:5-6 TPT
You become my delicious feast even when my enemies dare to fight. You anoint me with the fragrance of your Holy Spirit; you give me all I can drink of you until my heart overflows. So why would I fear the future? For your goodness and love pursue me all the days of my life.

Philippians 1:6-7 (TPT)
"I pray with great faith for you, because I'm fully convinced that the One who began this glorious work in you will faithfully continue the process of maturing you and will put his finishing touches to it until the unveiling or our Lord Jesus Christ! It's no wonder I pray with such confidence, since you have a permanent place in my heart"

Powerful Scriptures to Affirm Over Yourself

I AM God's child (1 Peter 1:23)

I AM God's temple (1 Corinthians 6:19-20)

I AM forgiven of all my sins (Ephesians 1:7)

I AM forever free from condemnation (Romans 8:1-2)

I AM assured that all things will work together for good

I AM chosen and appointed to bear fruit (John 15:16)

I AM holy and without blame before Him in love (Ephesians 1:7)

I AM righteousness of God in Christ (1 Corinthians 5:21)

I AM a partaker of His divine nature (2 Peter 1:4)

I AM healed (1 Peter 2:24)

 Dr. Diane Duckett a preacher, teacher, coach, motivational speaker and entrepreneur. Her passion for Jesus is an inspiration to those who want to grow deeper in their relationship with Christ and to know Him for themselves. Through prayer and living in full expectancy without limits, Dr. Diane is unleashing a vision and blazing a trail that will help others unleash and understand their full potential in the kingdom.

Dr. Diane is founder and Ladies Life, where she coaches women to live in full expectancy and to tap into their full potential by unleashing the vision God has given them for their lives. Her teachings inspire and challenge women to do better, to be better and to know better. She is also the founder and Business Owner of I AM Success Life Coach, LLC. As a certified Success and Transformational Life Coach, she helps individuals become a better successful individual in life and in business through her unique signature coaching program called "I AM Success," which was birth from her epic sign-off signature, "I AM Me!"

Dr. Diane believes that continuing education is important to her kingdom success. She holds a Bachelor of Science Degree in Business Management from the University of Phoenix, a Master of Divinity degree from the Howard University School of Divinity and a Doctor of Ministry degree in Transformational Leadership from Ashland Theological Seminary, Ashland, OH.

Dr. Diane is proud to be the wife of Dr. H. Duant'e Duckett of whom they are the proud parents of three beautiful children: DeAirra, Diamant'e, and Devin and five grandchildren, Aniya, Jrue, Dillian, Jayden and Summer.

CPSIA information can be obtained
at www.ICGtesting.com
Printed in the USA
JSHW060723210723
45142JS00010B/58